Copyright

Rose Garden Press
Suite #358 2055 Commercial Drive,
Vancouver, BC, Canada, V5N 0C7
https://gardentherapy.ca/

Published in Canada. 2018.

ISBN-13: 978-0-9950284-0-1

Rose, Stephanie.
The Natural Beauty Recipe Book; easy-to-make herbal skincare recipes for the whole body.
1. Beauty. —2. Crafts. —3. Bath & Body Care

Print Edition 14 13 12 11 10 / 10 9 8 7 6 5 4 3 2 1

Disclaimer

This book contains home recipes that have not been tested beyond personal use. The information in this book is not advice, and should not be treated as such. The information in this book is provided for informational purposes only.

While we do our best to provide useful information, any reliance you place on such information is strictly at your own risk and not a substitute for medical, legal, or any other professional advice of any kind.

What is written in this book is not intended to be substituted for the advice provided by your doctor or other healthcare professional. If you rely on any recipes or techniques, or use any of the products suggested or through the use of our website for decision making, without obtaining the advice of a physician or other healthcare professional, you do so at your own risk. The nutritional and other information in this book is not intended to be and does not constitute health care or medical advice.

The views expressed in this book have not been reviewed or endorsed by the FDA or any other private or public entity.

TABLE OF CONTENTS

INTRODUCTION 2

RESOURCES AND SUPPLIES 3

INGREDIENTS 5

SCRUBS, TONERS, & MASKS 12

BALMS & BUTTERS 22

TUB TIME! 36

SUMMER SKIN CARE 44

Introduction

Your body is a temple.

You are what you eat.

Garbage in, garbage out.

These are common phrases we often hear in regards to healthy living through natural food. The idea is that we are the result of the fuel that we put inside our bodies. Fill up with natural, healthy, nutritious ingredients and you can achieve health from the inside out.

I truly believe that garden-fresh produce, natural foods, and consuming only recognizable ingredients is the best way to be healthy inside. But what about our skin? Doesn't the same premise of "garbage in, garbage out" hold true? Don't the ingredients matter just as much when you use them on your outer layers?

Of course they do!

Your skin is an organ—the largest organ in your body—and it absorbs much of what we put onto it. If you eat healthy and treat your body like a temple, shouldn't you also be mindful of the ingredients that go on your skin?

Yes!

This book outlines some of my favorite recipes; the ones that I use every day with my family. By choosing ingredients that are close to nature, these skincare products have the power of healing from herbs and are so pure that (in most cases) you could eat them.

If you suffer from dry or oily skin, dry patches, blemishes, or other common skin issues, trying out the natural recipes in this book may make a world of difference for you.

There is more good news: natural beauty products are so much easier to make than you can imagine. Once you have the basic instructions and some ingredients you will spend only minutes mixing and melting your scrubs, lotions, and balms.

Many of the ingredients are likely in your kitchen right now. Others may be a little bit more elusive. But once you start stocking up on supplies you'll find that you spend far less money, use less packaging, make less polluting products, and change your skin forever.

Resources and Supplies

Before you get started on your natural beauty journey, I have created a resource and supplies page for this book:

https://gardentherapy.ca/natural-beauty-apothecary/

This page is meant to help you find everything from the ingredients to the tools you will need to get started at home. In many cases, you will already have everything you need in your kitchen. In other cases, you may need to order some of the supplies. Either way, it's best to stick to the recipes as they are written. Skincare is stricter than food recipes as not all substitutions will work.

The resources and supplies page is updated regularly to ensure that the items you need to make these projects can be found. You will also find links to the ingredients for each and every recipe found in this book, and in many cases, there will be a link to step-by-step photos if you need them. If you would like a bit more visual instruction, these links will help you get there.

You will also find DIY garden projects, plant-based beauty, green living, and inspirational garden tours over at Garden Therapy.

https://gardentherapy.ca/

Sign up for the FREE Garden Therapy Newsletter, What's in Season, to get a weekly update of seasonal projects, recipes, and articles that will help you live better through plants.

https://gardentherapy.ca/subscribe/

INGREDIENTS

OILS & BUTTERS...6

WAX 7

ESSENTIAL OILS...7

MANUKA HONEY 8

DRIED FLOWERS AND HERBS 8

NATURAL COLORANTS..9

INFUSED OILS...9

As with all home recipes, I recommend you test a bit on your skin and see how you react. Those with sensitivities, who are pregnant or breastfeeding, and who intend to use the recipes on children should take caution and check with their healthcare professional before making or using any homemade natural beauty recipes.

Oils & Butters

Olive Oil is probably the most common oil used in households, making it very easily accessible for use in natural beauty recipes. It is good at conditioning skin as well as being very stable. This rich yellow-to-green oil can have a strong aroma so it is often best mixed with other ingredients to make it more pleasant in skincare recipes. In the recipes in this book, it is not necessary to use virgin/extra virgin. Save the more expensive oil for cooking.

Jojoba Oil is listed here as oil, however it is technically a wax extracted from a Southwestern North American grown shrub (*Simmondsia chinensis*). Jojoba seeds are processed to produce a liquid wax ester that has similar skin absorption to our own sebum, making it an excellent carrier oil and cleanser.

Castor Oil is plant oil derived from the castor bean. It is most prominently used as an emollient in cosmetics. It is unique from other oils because it has water-binding properties that allow it to seal in moisture by creating a solid film on the skin.

Sweet Almond Oil is light, fragrant oil from the sweet almond. The oil is expeller pressed from almonds and contains the fatty acids and vitamins present in the nuts we eat. Sweet almond oil is popular in natural beauty recipes because it penetrates easily into the skin and thus it is effective at conditioning the skin and hair.

There is much written about the benefits of **Coconut Oil** on both diet and for use on the skin because of its high amount of fatty acids, antibacterial / antimicrobial properties, and its general ease of use. Many people use pure coconut oil, which is in a solid form at normal room temperature (76 F / 24 C), as a moisturizing lotion but it works even better when combined with other oils, waxes, and butters. When shopping for coconut oil for use in natural beauty recipes, it should be unrefined. Unlike olive oil, it is preferable to use virgin coconut oil.

Mango Butter has been used in Asia for centuries to moisturize skin. It is expeller pressed from mango seeds, full of essential fatty acids and vitamins, and melts on contact with skin.

Cocoa Butter is the edible fat extracted from the cocoa bean and the main ingredient in chocolate. In fact, the flavor and aroma of chocolate come from cocoa butter. True chocolate can only be called by name if it contains 100% cocoa butter. It is also full of antioxidants and is so good at moisturizing skin that it is very often used in skincare products. At room temperature, it is solid. But as you warm cocoa butter, the oil disperses into the other ingredients and blends well.

Shea Butter is another expeller-pressed fat with superior moisturizing properties for the skin. In addition, shea butter offers a low level of UV protection (approximately SPF-6). It has a somewhat strong aroma, so it is best mixed with other ingredients and scented with essential oils.

Wax

Beeswax is one of the most common waxes used in cosmetics as it is very effective at binding other ingredients and adding some solidity to the fats. Look for clean, cosmetic-grade beeswax sold in pellets or pastilles to save you the trouble of grating it. It also lends a gorgeous honey aroma to beauty products that makes it extra sweet.

Carnauba Wax is a very hard wax that comes from palm trees. Carnauba wax is also a good choice for vegan skincare recipes in place of beeswax.

Essential Oils

I use essential oils in all my homemade bath and body products as opposed to synthetic fragrance. There is much variety in quality and price of essential oils as there is no separate regulation for essential oils. The best way to get started with essential oils is to purchase a starter pack and start using them. Remember, essential oils should only be used with the approval of a healthcare practitioner.

Many of the recipes in this book only contain a few drops of an essential oil, which may make you question whether or not it is necessary. But with these small-batch recipes and the potency of essential oils, it really does make a world of difference to have even 1-2 drops.

Some of my favorite combinations are:

* lavender + grapefruit
* lemongrass + ginger
* rosemary + spearmint
* basil + bergamot
* sweet orange + vanilla + cinnamon
* lemon + lime + mandarin + sweet orange + pink grapefruit
* peppermint + vanilla (candy cane)

You will find plenty of recipe and scent recommendations in this book, but for more ideas on how to create a customized scent, skip forward to the recipe for Natural Solid Perfume and develop your own personalized scent combinations.

Manuka Honey

Manuka honey is collected from bees in New Zealand that pollinate manuka bushes. Look for raw organic honey with a UMF factor of 15 or more as this will have the most antibacterial properties. The antibacterial nature of honey comes from methylglyoxal (MG). MG is present in all honey but it can be found in much larger concentrations in manuka honey. Manuka honey also has anti-inflammatory properties, which is important when treating chapped or sun-damaged lips.

Dried Flowers and Herbs

Dried botanicals can add as much to a recipe as the other ingredients. Some can be used to infuse oils or make tea, while others can be added to a recipe for decorative or aesthetic properties. Ensure that if you are using dried botanicals that they are properly dried. Any remnants of moisture or mold spores will affect the end results of the recipes.

Some of the botanicals used in this book are:

- lavender
- chamomile
- calendula
- lemon balm
- peppermint
- rose
- *Monarda*
- *Centaurea*
- sunflower
- green tea

Natural Colorants

Ground-up, dried herbs and other organics work well as natural colors in your handmade beauty products. While you may not get the same bright hues as with synthetic colors, you will get natural tints and the peace of mind that what is going on your skin is good for you.

- ❋ Green – spirulina, sage powder
- ❋ Golden yellow – safflower powder
- ❋ Yellow – turmeric
- ❋ Orange (yellowish) – annatto seed powder
- ❋ Orange (reddish) – paprika
- ❋ Pink – madder root
- ❋ Purple – ratanjot
- ❋ Brown – cocoa powder

Infused Oils

Any recipe that uses infused oil with herbs is a great way to add color, scent, and healing properties to the raw ingredients you will be using in natural beauty recipes.

Simply soaking herbs in oil isn't enough to infuse the oil; it needs to be heated. Luckily, there are a few ways of doing this so you are sure to find one that suits your needs. The following describes how to infuse oils using the stove top, a slow cooker, or the sun!

The general instruction for all methods is to pack as many dried herbs as you can fit in a container, and then add in the oil so that the herbs are entirely submerged. Choose herbs that are completely dry (moisture and oil don't mix). When the infusing is finished, strain the herbs from the oil with a fine sieve once, then pour the oil through a coffee filter or cheesecloth-lined fine sieve.

Store the oil with a tight-fitting lid in a cool, dark place.

Generally, infused oil will last up to the "Best Before" date on the original package label. Olive oil should last for 2-3 years and coconut oil will last for many years, although spoiling could happen more quickly if contaminants were introduced in the infusing process.

Stove Top Oil Infusing

Use a double boiler to slowly heat the oil and herbs. Pack a handful of herbs in the top of a double boiler, and pour oil over. If you are using coconut oil, which is solid at room temperature, then melt the oil first and then add the herbs. Fill the bottom pot with an inch of water and set the double boiler on medium-low heat to warm up, then turn down to low for a few hours or until the oil becomes aromatic.

Slow Cooker Oil Infusing

The slow cooker method takes longer but it requires less attention than the other methods. Just set it and forget it!

If you have a small slow cooker, you can add the herbs right into the ceramic bowl and set it on low for 8-12 hours. To do a number of different herbs in separate oils, you can put the oil/herb combination in Mason jars and set those inside the slow cooker. Infuse for the same timing: 8-12 hours on low. There is no need to put lids on the jars when you have the lid on the slow cooker.

Sun-Infused Oil

Pack herbs into Mason jars and pour oil over them. Screw on a lid and set in the sun for 8 hours. The summer sun can be very hot, so this method is best used in cooler months and with large jars. Overheating the oils can remove some of the beneficial properties and this method is one you will have to watch more closely. It doesn't use any power beyond the sun so you can infuse oils right out in the garden as you harvest them!

Infused oils can be substituted in most recipes for natural beauty that call for oil: soap, body butter, lip balm, and scrubs. Some good choices for oils to infuse are olive oil, coconut oil, and sweet almond oil. Herbs that are good for infusing are:

* Lavender – relaxing, antibacterial, adds purple color to oil
* Calendula – healing, adds golden color to oil
* Chamomile – calming
* Comfrey – helps with pain and inflammation
* Sage – pain relief, anti-inflammatory
* Sunflower – anti-inflammatory, adds yellow color to oil
* Mint – energizing, pain relieving, darkens color of oil
* Rose – romance, love, adds pink color to oil
* Lemon balm – calming, increasing circulation

SCRUBS, TONERS, & MASKS

SUPER SIMPLE SUGAR SCRUB 13

LEMON MERINGUE SUGAR SCRUB 14

HEALING HIMALAYAN PINK SALT SCRUB 15

HONEY LIP SCRUB 16

PAMPERING PEPPERMINT FOOT SCRUB 17

HOMEMADE TONER RECIPES 18

FOODIE FACE MASKS 19

ALL-NATURAL HAND SANITIZER RECIPE 20

Super Simple Sugar Scrub

An uber-moisturizing, exfoliating sugar scrub recipe that will wake up your skin and your mind with two energizing scent choices: lemongrass and ginger or rosemary and spearmint.

INGREDIENTS

Makes 1 ½ cups

- ❋ Small 4 oz jam jars
- ❋ 1 cup granulated white sugar
- ❋ ¾ cup sweet almond oil

Lemongrass Ginger Recipe Ingredients

- ❋ 3 drops lemongrass essential oil
- ❋ 1 drop ginger essential oil
- ❋ ¼ tsp turmeric for color

Rosemary Spearmint Recipe Ingredients

- ❋ 2 drops rosemary essential oil
- ❋ 2 drops spearmint essential oil
- ❋ ¼ tsp spirulina for color
- ❋ ¼ tsp crushed dried mint leaves

MAKE IT!

In a bowl or large measuring cup, mix together the sugar, oil and recipe ingredients. Spoon the mixture into small jam jars and smooth out the top.

Lemon Meringue Sugar Scrub

The delicious scent of lemon and vanilla together will brighten your mind and awaken your appetite.

INGREDIENTS

Makes ½ cup

- ☀ ½ cup white sugar
- ☀ ¼ cup lemon balm infused olive oil
- ☀ 3-4 drops vanilla absolute (essential oil)
- ☀ 5-6 drops lemon essential oil

MAKE IT!

Mix all ingredients in a bowl thoroughly.

Note: Vanilla absolute is different than vanilla extract - please use the absolute as it is much more concentrated. As it is quite dark, it will add a bit of brown to your sugar scrub, so only use a few drops. Those drops do go a long way in giving this scrub a delicious scent and it helps to mask the olive oil aroma.

If you aren't a fan of olive oil, you can substitute it for the same amount of coconut oil or sweet almond oil. If you swap out the oil, your scrub will also be white.

Healing Himalayan Pink Salt Scrub

This Himalayan pink salt scrub is a powerful detoxifier packed with healing minerals for your whole body. With rose petals and essential oils added, this scrub becomes a home spa treatment that heals, soothes, and revitalizes the skin.

There are many benefits to using Himalayan pink salt as a culinary ingredient, as it is full of 80+ minerals and elements such as magnesium, calcium, and potassium. The pink color is a result of these trace elements in the salt, including energy-rich iron. These minerals can often be more accessible to the body through dermal absorption, making this salt scrub a nourishing and therapeutic experience for the body.

Rose geranium, pink grapefruit, and ylang-ylang essential oils have been added for an aroma that helps to bring balance and harmony as well as stimulating and uplifting properties. This powerful combination works wonders to transform a weary body and mind in just the time it takes to have a bath.

INGREDEINTS

Makes 1 cup

- ✳ 1 cup pink Himalayan sea salt
- ✳ ¼ cup coconut oil
- ✳ 2 tbsp sweet almond oil
- ✳ 10 drops rose geranium essential oil
- ✳ 5 drops pink grapefruit essential oil
- ✳ 5 drops ylang-ylang essential oil
- ✳ Dried rose petals (optional)

MAKE IT!

Mix together all ingredients except rose petals in a jar. Warm up the coconut oil if you need to soften it. Add dried rose petals to the top of the jar if you want a more luxurious bath or if giving it as a gift. Store in small batches in the fridge to prolong life.

DIRECTIONS FOR USE

This Himalayan pink salt scrub is best when applied before a warm bath. Massage into wet skin all over the body and step into a warm bath for at least 20 minutes. Soak, rest, relax, and dry skin after the bath. Bring a cool glass of water to the bath with you as detoxification can be powerful.

Honey Lip Scrub

Keep lips kissable and soft with this healing honey sugar scrub. Summer sun, cold winter air, and everything in between can cause chapped, dry, or inflamed lips but with this recipe you can say goodbye to dry, chapped lips forever! Honey is a natural antibacterial, sugar scrubs off any dry skin, and the oils moisturize.

INGREDIENTS

Makes 3 tablespoons

* ½ tsp manuka honey
* ½ tsp olive oil
* 2 tbsp sugar

MAKE IT!

Mix all ingredients together well and store in a small, airtight container.

Apply a pea-sized amount to lips and massage in until the sugar has dissolved. Rinse with cool water and a cloth. Apply the lip balm of your choice (many natural recipes can be found in this book.)

Store in the fridge for up to 30 days.

Pampering Peppermint Foot Scrub

What do achy, dry, rough feet need? A little pampering! This peppermint sugar scrub is made for feet. Exfoliating sugar and dried herbs will scrub away rough skin, coconut oil will soften cracks, and soothing peppermint essential oil will help to ease pain.

This recipe is perfect for feet. You can certainly use it all over your body, and I have, but I love this for cooling and soothing feet. The secret is in the peppermint essential oil. It has analgesic and anti-inflammatory properties to relieve pain and inflammation. It also has a stimulating and cooling effect on the skin that can really perk up tired feet. If you are prone to foot or leg cramps, peppermint essential oil's anti-spasmodic properties can help with that too!

INGREDIENTS

Makes 1 cup

- ✳ 2/3 cup white sugar
- ✳ 1/2 cup coconut oil
- ✳ 8-10 drops peppermint essential oil
- ✳ 1/2 tsp dried herbs such as mint, lavender, chamomile

MAKE IT!

Coconut oil is a solid at room temperature so it will require melting beforehand. Measure sugar into a Mason jar, then pour melted coconut oil in. Add essential oil drops and stir well.

Add in dried herbs for additional texture and for visual appeal. I like to use dried mint, lavender, and chamomile from the garden.

Tip: If you don't have dried herbs handy you can use the contents of a mint tea bag.

Homemade Toner Recipes

A toner helps to balance skin's pH level after cleansing. Soap is typically alkaline and a toner helps to bring the skin back to a neutral pH which helps to prevent blemishes and signs of aging.

GREEN TEA TONER

Use this toner to tighten up skin and reduce the signs of aging.

- 1 cup green tea
- 1 tbsp rosewater

CHAMOMILE TONER

This toner is great to calm inflamed, red skin.

- 1 cup chamomile tea
- 1 tbsp witch hazel

APPLE CIDER VINEGAR TONER

This toner balances out blemish-prone skin.

- 1 cup water
- ¼ cup apple cider vinegar

MAKE IT!

Mix ingredients together and add to spray bottle. Spritz skin after cleansing. Pat to dry.

Foodie Face Masks

Simple face masks can be made with any number of fresh foods found in your refrigerator.

BASIC FACE MASK RECIPE

Mix together 1 tbsp of each yogurt and honey and apply to face.

Add in these foods for additional benefits

- ❋ 1/2 of an avocado, mashed (moisturizing)
- ❋ 1 carrot, boiled, mashed, and cooled (repairs skin tissue)
- ❋ 1 small banana, mashed (brightens skin)
- ❋ 5 strawberries, hulled and mashed (balances oily skin)
- ❋ ½ cucumber, puréed (soothes skin)
- ❋ ¼ cup prepared oatmeal (helps skin retain moisture)
- ❋ Aloe vera gel (soothes rashes and burns)

MAKE IT!

Mix together. Stir and apply to face. Let sit 15-20 minutes and wash off. These recipes do not store well so discard leftovers.

All-Natural Hand Sanitizer Recipe

Thieves Oil is an essential oil blend of clove, lemon, cinnamon, eucalyptus, and rosemary.

The story behind this blend is that a band of 15th-century thieves remained in tip-top health despite ransacking riches from the graves of those who had died from the bubonic plague.

When they were captured, they were traded leniency in their sentence for sharing the secret to their impervious health. So the legend of Thieves Oil was born.

Whether you believe the story or not, the benefits of essential oils in boosting immunity and countering germs is much more plausible.

I personally prefer a homemade product over one filled with ingredients I don't recognize and hand sanitizer is one of those products that I love to have a more natural version of.

That being said, please recognize that essential oils are potent and can be harmful to some. Thieves Oil contains clove, rosemary, and eucalyptus oils which are not safe for use on small children. Use this hand sanitizer on grown-ups only, please. You can replace clove, rosemary and eucalyptus oils with lavender, sweet orange, and fir oils if you plan to use it around children 6 months and older (no essential oils are recommended for babies younger than 6 months old).

You can buy a Thieves Oil blend or make your own for this recipe.

INGREDIENTS

Makes 1 cup
* 1/3 cup pure witch hazel
* 2/3 cup 100% pure aloe vera gel
* 1 capsule of Vitamin E oil – a natural preservative
* 15 drops Thieves essential oil blend
  or Homemade Thieves Oil Recipe
    * 10 drops clove essential oil
    * 9 drops lemon essential oil
    * 5 drops cinnamon essential oil
    * 4 drops eucalyptus essential oil
    * 3 drops rosemary essential oil

MAKE IT!

Mix witch hazel and aloe vera gel together well in a bowl.

Add essential oils and mix well, then open the vitamin E capsule and empty that into the gel.

Use a funnel to pour it into a pump, tube, or another container.

Shake well before each use. Squeeze a dime-sized amount on the palm of your hand and massage in.

 It will feel sticky at first but it will absorb cleanly in no time.

Your hands will feel dry, clean, and smell terrific.

BALMS & BUTTERS

MAKING BALMS...24

BASIC LIP BALM RECIPE..25

CHOCOLATE MINT LIP BALM...27

TROPICAL CITRUS & COCONUT LIP GLOSS 28

HEALING CUTICLE BALM 29

NATURAL SOLID PERFUME 30

CALENDULA HEALING SALVE 31

ALL-NATURAL VAPOR RUB RECIPE 32

MANGO CITRUS WHIPPED BODY BUTTER 33

Making Balms

Balms are a mixture of fats and waxes to create fairly solid forms of moisturizer. Making balms is a simple process of melting the ingredients together and pouring them into a container. Specific instructions are outlined here, with recipes for different balms to follow.

EQUIPMENT

- ❋ Double boiler or Turkish coffee pot
- ❋ Small spatula or metal spoon
- ❋ Lip balm tubes, metal tins, or pots

MAKE IT!

Note: it really helps if you have a double boiler where the top pot has a pour spout. If not, you can transfer the hot liquid into a measuring cup with a spout for easier pouring.

Melt the oils and waxes in a double boiler.

Remove from heat, add essential oils, and blend with a small spatula or metal spoon while the mixture cools but is still pourable.

If you are using tins or pots, pour the hot liquid into the container and leave untouched until set.

If you are using tubes, fill each tube halfway and let cool slightly. This will set the bottom of the tube so that a hole doesn't form at the top of the lip balm when cooled. Before the tubes are starting to set, fill the rest of the way, so there is a convex curve on the top, being careful not to spill over the edges. When the lip balm cools, it will shrink so it should end up having a flat top. If you need to even out the top, a heat gun works really well.

Now that you have a handle on how to make a balm, let's move on to the recipes!

Basic Lip Balm Recipe

This is a basic recipe for lip balm that has the right balance of oil and wax to both moisturize and protect your lips. Add any combination of essential oils to this recipe to make your signature creation.

INGREDIENTS

Makes 12 tubes

* 4 tbsp castor oil
* 4 tsp beeswax pellets
* 1 tsp carnauba wax
* 16-20 drops essential oil
* Variation: add ¼ tsp of manuka honey for shine
* Variation: add ¼ tsp of cocoa or cranberry powder for color

MAKE IT!

Measure all the ingredients into a small double boiler or a Turkish coffee pot. I like to use the Turkish coffee pot because it has a pour spout. I can heat the oils up quickly and then pour them easily into the tubes.

Once the oils, waxes, and butter have all melted together turn off the heat and add in the essential oils. Stir well with a small spatula.

When everything is thoroughly mixed, use the spout on the Turkish coffee pot to pour the lip balm into the tubes. Fill each tube to just above where the center screw is.

Let the lip balm cool and then warm up the remaining mixture in the pot so that you can top off each one of the tubes.

Filling the lip balm tubes in two steps ensures that you won't have a large depressed area with a hole in the center of the lip balm. If this still happens then you can always add a little bit more lip balm onto the top of the depressed area and use a lighter to melt it onto the rest of the lip balm.

If this recipe is just for your own use (and you don't really care what it looks like) then simply fill up each one of the tubes the first time; it won't affect the final product's function or usefulness.

HEALING EUCALYPTUS LIP BALM

This healing balm is an anti-inflammatory and soothing recipe for lips that are very dry and/or chapped. Peppermint and eucalyptus cool lips and reduce inflammation while lavender acts as an antibacterial and antifungal to protect lips.

To make this variation, add the following to the basic recipe:

* ❋ 10 drops peppermint essential oil
* ❋ 5 drops eucalyptus essential oil
* ❋ 5 drops lavender essential oil

CHAI LIP BALM

Chai lip balm is filled with spices that wake you up and make your lips tingle. This recipe is spicy and will encourage blood flow to the lips, making them fuller and rosy. If you have sensitive lips, use half the essential oils and/or avoid using this lip balm if you don't like the sensation.

To make this variation, add the following to the basic recipe:

* ❋ 8 drops cinnamon essential oil
* ❋ 8 drops vanilla absolute essential oil
* ❋ 4 drops clove essential oil
* ❋ 2 drops ginger essential oil
* ❋ Optional: ¼ tsp cocoa powder

CANDY CANE LIP BALM

This festive recipe smells just like the holidays! Candy cane scented lip balm gives you a minty tingle along with a sweet vanilla aroma that will make it an everyday favorite.

To make this variation, add the following to the basic recipe:

* ❋ 16 drops peppermint essential oil
* ❋ 10 drops vanilla essential oil

Chocolate Mint Lip Balm

This lip balm is a luscious treat for the chocolate lover without any of those pesky calories. Cocoa butter is ultra-moisturizing and because it melts at body temperature, it is readily absorbed into the skin. The mint essential oils will add a cooling tingle to this luxurious lip butter.

INGREDIENTS

Makes 4 pots or 10 tubes

- ✳ 1 tbsp cocoa butter
- ✳ 1 tbsp sweet almond oil
- ✳ 1 tbsp castor oil
- ✳ 1 tbsp grated beeswax
- ✳ ½ tsp carnauba wax
- ✳ 8 drops peppermint essential oil
- ✳ 7 drops spearmint essential oil
- ✳ Optional: ¼ tsp cocoa powder

MAKE IT!

Melt the cocoa butter, oils and waxes in a double boiler.

Remove from heat, add essential oils and cocoa powder, and blend well.

Keep stirring as you pour the lip balm into tubes as the cocoa will settle quickly.

Leave untouched to set.

Tropical Citrus & Coconut Lip Gloss

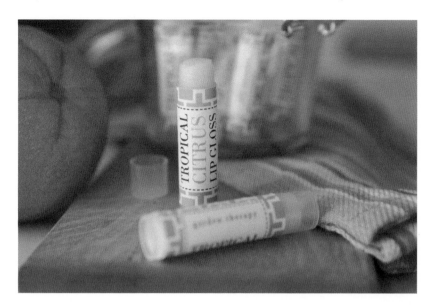

This is an uplifting lip balm with tropical coconut oil that glides on lips smoothly. Coconut oil is a natural bacteria fighting oil and is full of antioxidants to help prevent aging. This is a softer lip balm so it is perfect for everyday wear.

INGREDIENTS

Makes 4 pots or 10 tubes

- ✳ 1 tbsp coconut oil
- ✳ 1 tbsp sweet almond oil
- ✳ 1 tbsp castor oil
- ✳ 1 tbsp grated beeswax
- ✳ 1 tsp carnauba wax
- ✳ 10 drops sweet orange essential oil
- ✳ 5 drops ylang-ylang essential oil

MAKE IT!

Melt the cocoa butter, oils, and waxes in a double boiler. Remove from heat, add essential oils, and blend well. Pour into tubes and leave untouched to set.

Healing Cuticle Balm

Home chefs, gardeners, and just about anyone in cold climates during the winter will regularly have problems with dry, cracked cuticles. This soothing balm is packed with an herbal blend that will mend those cracks and make cuticles soft again.

INGREDIENTS

Makes 5 small lip balm pots or 2 larger pots

- ❋ 1 tbsp coconut oil
- ❋ 1 tbsp sweet almond oil
- ❋ 1 tbsp hemp oil
- ❋ 1 tbsp mango butter
- ❋ 1½ tbsp grated beeswax
- ❋ 10 drops lavender essential oil
- ❋ 5 drops peppermint essential oil
- ❋ 5 drops eucalyptus essential oil
- ❋ 5 drops fennel essential oil
- ❋ 5 drops clary sage essential oil

MAKE IT!

Melt the butter, oils, and wax in a double boiler. Remove from heat, add essential oils, and blend well. Pour into pots and leave untouched to set.

Natural Solid Perfume

Here is where you get to play with scents you love to come up with your own signature scent. A good place to start is with your nose! Choose a scent that you know you love (Lavender? Vanilla? Citrus?) and choose another essential oil that you think will match well. Unscrew the caps and hold them to your nose. Add more scents until you have the right mix and your signature scent is born!

INGREDIENTS

Makes 5 small lip balm pots or 2 larger pots

- ❊ 3 tbsp jojoba oil or sweet almond oil
- ❊ 1 tbsp unrefined coconut oil
- ❊ 1 tbsp beeswax pellets
- ❊ 50 drops essential oil

MAKE IT!

Melt the oils and wax in a double boiler.

Remove from heat, add essential oils, and blend well.

Pour into pots and leave untouched to set.

Calendula Healing Salve

This moisturizing calendula salve helps soothe and heal cuts and bruises and is safe to use on adults, children, and pets.

INGREDIENTS AND MATERIALS

Makes 2 x 2 oz tins of salve

* 1/4 cup olive oil infused with calendula flowers
* 1 tbsp jojoba oil
* 2 tsp shea butter
* 2 tsp grated beeswax
* 1 tsp cocoa butter
* 1 tsp carnauba wax
* Double boiler
* 2 x 2 oz shallow metal tins

MAKE IT!

Infuse olive oil with calendula flowers as described in the Ingredients chapter. In a double boiler, slowly heat up the olive oil and the remaining ingredients until just melted. Stir well. Pour into the metal tins and allow to cool completely before use.

TO USE

Apply the salve to scrapes or cuts to speed up healing. This can also be used as a lip balm on chapped lips and as a cuticle balm on dry cuticles.

All-Natural Vapor Rub Recipe

When you are hit with a cold and need a little relief from chest pain and cough there is nothing like eucalyptus and menthol, similar to active ingredients in commercially purchased vapor rubs.

INGREDIENTS

Makes 3 x 4 oz tins

- ✳ 1/2 cup comfrey infused olive oil
- ✳ 1 cup coconut oil
- ✳ 3/4 cup grated beeswax
- ✳ 35 drops eucalyptus essential oil
- ✳ 30 drops peppermint essential oil
- ✳ 15 drops lavender essential oil
- ✳ 15 drops rosemary essential oil

MAKE IT!

Melt the oils and wax over a double boiler. Stir in essential oils. Pour into metal tins and let set. Re-melt to add more essential oils if you want it a bit stronger.

TO USE

Rub balm on your chest to help soothe congestion and cough. Rub under your nose for a stuffy nose and sore skin from scratchy tissues. Have someone rub some on your feet just because it feels good to get a foot rub when you have a rotten cold.

Mango Citrus Whipped Body Butter

A perfectly light and silky butter that's more like whipped cream. The uplifting citrus scent plus the healing properties of mango and shea butter make this the perfect lotion for soothing dry skin after the shower. It also has just the right texture for massage so consider this as a gift for someone who could use a little pampering.

INGREDIENTS

Makes 2 x 4 oz jam jars

- ✳ 1 ½ tbsp mango butter
- ✳ 1 ½ tbsp cocoa butter
- ✳ 2 tbsp shea butter
- ✳ 2 tbsp coconut oil
- ✳ 1 ½ tbsp apricot kernel oil
- ✳ 20 drops citrus essential oil: 5 lime, 5 sweet orange, 5 lemon, 5 pink grapefruit

EQUIPMENT

- ✳ Double boiler
- ✳ Metal spoon
- ✳ 2 small glass jam jars (4 oz each)
- ✳ Digital kitchen scale
- ✳ Whisk or electric hand mixer
- ✳ Ice water bath

MAKE IT!

Measure all of the ingredients then add the oils and butters into the double boiler. Gently melt, not letting the mixture get too hot.

Set up the ice water bath by adding water and ice to a bowl large enough for the top pot of the double boiler to fit in. When the oils and butter are melted, move the pot to the ice bath and stir in the essential oils.

When the mixture is beginning to cool, whip until stiff peaks form. This will happen quickly when the butter is cool enough.

Scoop the whipped butter into two clean glass jars and seal airtight. Use within a few months as there are no preservatives to prevent spoiling. Add the contents of a few vitamin E tablets before whipping for a slightly more extended shelf life.

TUB TIME!

EASY LAVENDER LEMON BALM BATH SALTS..37

GARDENER'S HERBAL FOOT SOAK 38

BATH BOMBS..39

TUB TEA..41

LAVENDER AND COCOA BUTTER BATH MELTS..42

Easy Lavender Lemon Balm Bath Salts

Making fragrant jars of homemade bath salts couldn't be easier. In vintage canning jars, bath salts look beautiful on display and make wonderful gifts.

INGREDIENTS AND MATERIALS

* Epsom salts
* 10-15 drops lavender essential oil
* 1 heaping tablespoon dried lavender and lemon balm leaves
* Vintage canning jars

MAKE IT!

Fill each canning jar about halfway full of the Epsom salts. Add the essential oil, replace lid, and shake. Remove the lid again, add dried botanicals, replace lid and shake (again). Add more Epsom salts to fill the jar and then (you guessed it) replace the lid and shake shake shake.

Gardener's Herbal Foot Soak

This herbal soak looks pretty in the jar but packs a powerful punch of herbs in a foot bath: eucalyptus, rosemary, and comfrey root powder to soothe aches, lavender to relax, and mint to refresh. Why should feet have all the fun? It's a great soak for use in the bath as well.

INGREDIENTS

Makes 2 cups

- 2 cups Epsom salts
- 8 drops lavender essential oil
- 6 drops mint essential oil
- 2 drops eucalyptus essential oil
- 2 drops rosemary essential oil
- 1 tsp dried comfrey root powder
- 1 tsp dried lavender
- 1 tsp dried mint leaves
- ¼ tsp dried *Centaurea* and *Monarda* petals for color

MAKE IT!

Fill a pretty jar about halfway full of the Epsom salts. Add essential oils and botanicals, replace lid, and shake. Add more Epsom salts to fill the jar, replace the lid and shake one last time.

Bath Bombs

Love those awesome fizzing bath bombs but don't want to spend $6 a piece? It's easy to make your own with natural ingredients.

While there are many other recipes that recommend using synthetic fragrance and coloring, there are plenty of options available that are 100% natural. You can feel confident that when you use these natural products or give them as gifts, that they are healthy for the body.

INGREDIENTS AND MATERIALS

Makes 12 medium bath bombs

- ❋ 2 cups baking soda
- ❋ 1 cup citric acid
- ❋ 100% pure witch hazel
- ❋ Spray bottle
- ❋ 10-20 drops of essential oils
- ❋ Natural colorant
- ❋ Plastic molds

MAKE IT!

In a large bowl, measure in the baking soda and citric acid and mix well.

Add ½ teaspoon of coloring and mix well. Add more coloring if you want a deeper color, but keep in mind that too much color will leave a ring in your tub, so go easy. The color will become more pronounced when you add the witch hazel anyhow.

Add 20-30 drops of essential oils and mix well.

Using an atomizer or spray bottle filled with which hazel, lightly spray the entire surface of the powder and mix with your hands at the same time. Keep spraying and mixing rapidly until the mixture holds together when scrunched with your hand (think of making snowballs). Be careful not to add to much witch hazel – a little goes a long way.

Working quickly, firmly press mixture into molds. You can use soap-making molds, chocolate molds, ice cube trays, or even plastic Christmas ornaments that snap into two parts. The key is that they are plastic and large enough for the bath bomb to combine and set.

Gently tap the mold so that the bath bomb releases and carefully lay on a towel or tray to dry. To make a round bath bomb, over-fill two molds and press them together firmly before tapping the mold to release the bath bomb.

Let the bath bombs dry for 30 minutes or until they are firm and won't fall apart.

Tip: use the extra powder from the bowl and counter and shake it into carpets or rugs, then vacuum. Instant deodorizing!

Tub Tea

Herbs are fabulous in the bath but they can leave a lot of mess behind. Tub teas can contain herbs, salts, moisturizers, and skin softeners to create a soothing bath without all the cleanup.

To make a tub tea, start with extra-large paper tea bags, then choose your ingredients. Here is a list of some of the possible options:

* Dried lavender
* Rose petals
* Pink Himalayan bath salts
* Epsom salts
* Ground oatmeal
* Dried monarda (bee balm)
* Dried mint leaves
* Fennel seeds
* Comfrey root powder
* Powdered milk or goat's milk

MAKE IT!

Seal the tea bags by folding the top down 4-5 times and secure with a single staple.

Pack tea bags into a Mason jar or pretty vase and give with instructions to use.

Lavender and Cocoa Butter Bath Melts

Add a little luxury to the bath with these moisturizing cocoa butter bath melts. They are made with ingredients so natural that you could eat them, and you might just want to! The cocoa, coconut, lavender aroma makes my mouth water for what is essentially a truffle. These truffles are best used in the bath, however, as the silky soft oils melt in the warm water and soak into your skin.

INGREDIENTS AND MATERIALS

Makes 12 bath melts

* ¼ cup cocoa butter
* 2 tbsp coconut oil
* 20 drops lavender essential oil
* 1 tbsp dried lavender flowers
* Turkish coffee pot
* Spatula
* Silicone ice cube tray as a mold

MAKE IT!

Melt the oils in the small pot over medium-low heat. Stir constantly and keep a watchful eye on the oils. You want them to just reach the melting point and not overheat.

When the oils have melted and combined, add the essential oils and stir well.

Immediately pour into silicone molds. I used a silicone ice-cube tray but a candy mold will also work. A small pot with a pour spout makes this job a lot easier. I use a Turkish coffee pot for all my natural skincare recipes as it is small but tall, has a long handle to keep your hands away from hot oils, and because it is much easier to pour with a spout.

Sprinkle dried lavender buds on the hot oil, dividing the tablespoon up evenly between the bath melts.

Move the silicone mold to the refrigerator to cool for 2 hours. Store the finished bath melts in the fridge or a cool place if your house is warm so they don't melt before you want to use them!

Pop one or two bath melts into a tub filled with hot water and soak for at least 20 minutes.

SUMMER SKIN CARE

ABOUT NATURAL SUN PROTECTION 45

SUNSCREEN LIP BALM 46

AFTER-SUN LIP BALM 47

ALOE VERA SUNBURN REMEDY 48

AFTER-SUN SALVE RECIPE 49

ALL-NATURAL BUG SPRAY 50

INSECT BITE ROLL-ON REMEDY 51

About Natural Sun Protection

Making sunscreen or sun protection products at home is an easy way to add sun protection into your normal beauty routine. Many ingredients that are used in natural beauty recipes provide a degree of SPF. Raspberry seed oil (natural SPF of 28-50) and carrot seed essential oil (SPF can be as high as 40) are commonly used in sun protection recipes. Wheat germ oil and jojoba oils, as well as shea butter, all have SPF properties.

Even so, I would not venture a guess as to what the SPF is of a homemade recipe.

My general rule of thumb is to stay out of the sun when the UV is strongest and take the steps to protect my skin (and lips) as naturally as possible.

In the hottest and sunniest days of the year, I use a store-bought natural sunscreen on my fair, freckly skin if I must be in the sun. The sun is no joke these days and I need to cover myself in some solid sun protection when the sun is at its peak. In most cases, I stay in the shade, cover up with clothes, and stay indoors during the hottest hours mid-day. But during the rest of the year, the natural SPF in homemade recipes is enough to keep me protected.

It's important to also note that there are ingredients that can cause the sun's effects to be accelerated. Phototoxic essential oils typically run in the citrus family (lemon, lime, bitter orange, mandarin leaf, and grapefruit). Sweet orange oil, however, is generally considered not phototoxic.

The recipes in this chapter are great to have on hand in the summer to soothe skin that has had sun exposure as well as to prevent or soothe bug bites.

So cover up, swap out the citrus, and then go out and have some fun in the sun!

Sunscreen Lip Balm

Applying sunscreen meant for your skin directly to your lips doesn't taste very good. Plus it dries out your lips and dulls the shine. Instead, try this homemade sun protection lip balm, it will protect your lips, make them kissably soft, and it's made of all-natural ingredients.

INGREDIENTS

Makes 6 tubes

- ✳ 2 tbsp olive oil with calendula
- ✳ 1 tbsp jojoba oil
- ✳ 1 tbsp wheat germ oil
- ✳ ½ tsp raspberry seed oil
- ✳ 2 tbsp grated beeswax
- ✳ 1½ tsp carnauba wax
- ✳ 1 tsp shea butter
- ✳ 10 drops vanilla essential oil
- ✳ 8 drops sweet orange essential oil
- ✳ 5 drops carrot seed essential oil

MATERIALS

- ✳ 6 lip balm tubes
- ✳ Turkish coffee pot or small double boiler
- ✳ Small spatula

MAKE IT!

Follow the instructions to make lip balm from the Balms and Butters chapter.

After-Sun Lip Balm

Did you know that your lips can get sunburned? Of course they can! But you may not think about it when you slather on that SPF. In case you forgot about the skin on your lips, here is a healing after-sun recipe to cool and soothe sunburned lips.

INGREDIENTS

Makes 6 tubes

* 2 tbsp calendula infused olive oil
* 2 tbsp castor oil
* 2 tbsp grated beeswax
* 1 ½ tsp carnauba wax
* 1 tsp shea butter
* 10 drops vanilla essential oil
* 8 drops ylang-ylang essential oil
* 5 drops peppermint essential oil
* 5 drops lavender essential oil

MATERIALS

* 6 lip balm tubes
* Turkish coffee pot or small double boiler
* Small spatula

MAKE IT!

Follow the instructions to make lip balm from the Balms and Butters chapter.

Aloe Vera Sunburn Remedy

The healing power of plants cannot be denied, especially when something as simple as an aloe vera plant can provide great relief to something so painful: sunburned skin. This aloe vera sunburn remedy is one that I have been using for as many years as I can remember.

Aloe vera is a powerful anti-inflammatory and it is most potent when applied directly from the plant.

MAKE IT!

Cut a piece of aloe vera off of the plant with a sharp knife. Cut the tip off of one of the leaves (it can be as large as the majority of the leaf or just part of the tip). Cut at an angle and don't cut the whole leaf so the end of the leaf will seal up. Then take a paring knife and split the leaf in half so that the gel inside has the most surface area. Take the leaf and rub it directly on the burn*. You can also put the leaves in the fridge and use them as a cold gel to soothe the burn. It will feel good but will not add any additional healing properties so this isn't an essential step.

*Be sure to test a small patch of skin before applying it everywhere. Some people have allergies to aloe vera straight from the plant and you don't want to cause a bad reaction!

Compost the leaves when you're finished applying the gel on your skin and repeat every six hours if you're still looking for a relief from a nasty sunburn. Please note that this is for a typical sunburn, serious burns with blisters, headache, or severe pain should be seen by a doctor.

After-Sun Salve Recipe

Even if you don't have a sunburn, this after-sun salve is a summer necessity to rehydrate and soothe sun-kissed skin. Apply it after a good scrub in the shower to remove sunscreen residue. Slather on this salve and your skin will drink in the oils and butters, dealing with sun-damaged skin while you sleep.

INGREDIENTS

Makes 2 oz

- ❋ 3 tbsp olive oil infused with calendula (see Ingredients chapter)
- ❋ 1 tbsp coconut oil
- ❋ 1 tsp cocoa butter
- ❋ 1 tsp shea butter
- ❋ 1 tbsp grated beeswax
- ❋ 15 drops lavender essential oil
- ❋ 3 tbsp aloe vera gel at room temperature

MAKE IT!

Melt the oils, butters, and beeswax in a double boiler or Turkish coffee pot. Use a medium heat and stir as the oils melt. Remove from heat just as all ingredients are liquid. Stir in essential oil. Allow to cool slightly and then add the aloe gel. Mix the gel in well with the rest and pour into a 2oz container.

TO USE

Apply the salve generously to sunburned skin and rub it in as well as you can (which I know can be difficult with a sunburn!). Apply again after waking in the morning or showering, until the sunburn has settled down. Shower to remove any sunscreen and use the salve each evening after a day of sun exposure.

All-Natural Bug Spray

This all-natural bug spray recipe is not only bad for bugs, it's good for you. Good because it's super simple. Good because it actually smells nice. And good because it's not toxic on your skin. All that and it keeps mosquitoes from biting. This recipe uses some pleasing essential oils in a base of witch hazel that you'll love and they hate.

INGREDIENTS

- ✳ 4 drops citronella essential oil
- ✳ 4 drops lemongrass essential oil
- ✳ 4 drops rosemary essential oil
- ✳ 4 drops eucalyptus essential oil
- ✳ 4 drops mint essential oil
- ✳ 1/4 cup pure witch hazel

MAKE IT!

Add all ingredients into a small glass or plastic atomizer. Shake well and apply liberally.

Insect Bite Roll-On Remedy

This insect bite roll-on is great to have on hand when you least expect that you'll get attacked by mosquitoes, flies, or other annoying pests. If you've ever been caught outside at dusk without bug spray you may also know the frustration of trying to enjoy time with friends while getting eaten alive by mosquitoes or swarmed by flies. This handy little roll-on bottle is an easy way to make sure that you always have a bite relief on hand in your purse, pocket, or bag.

INGREDIENTS AND MATERIALS

* 10ml glass aromatherapy roll-on bottle
* Small funnel
* Pure witch hazel
* 2 drops lavender essential oil
* 2 drops tea tree essential oil

MAKE IT!

Pour the witch hazel into the roll-on bottle using a small funnel. Add the essential oils and put the roll-on top back on the bottle. Shake well before using.

To quickly relieve mosquito bites, apply the roll-on as soon as you see the bite or feel it starting to itch. Don't scratch! Roll on a little of this bug-bite relief right onto the bite and allow it to dry. Again, don't scratch!

The more you scratch the more inflamed it will be. If you can restrain yourself while the bug-bite remedy works, you should feel better in about 15 minutes.

About the Author

Stephanie Rose is an award-winning author and the creator of Garden Therapy (https://gardentherapy.ca). Garden Therapy started as a personal blog and has bloomed into a community of craft and garden projects for people looking to add some creativity to their lives.

Originally, Stephanie started writing as a way to log her garden therapy journey while recovering from a sudden and debilitating illness. She soon connected with others who also used gardening and craft projects as therapy and shifted the blog to focus on sharing clear and helpful do-it-yourself instructions for over 800 healthy living, gardening, and craft projects.

Stephanie started making her own natural beauty products and soap in 2008 to use what was growing in the garden for personal beauty and wellness. After testing countless recipes, she has found what works best for her family and now makes all of her own soaps, lotions, scrubs, lip balms, and healing salves. Stephanie is an avid soap-maker and makes both cold-process soap and melt-and-pour soap recipes.

Stephanie lives in Vancouver, BC, where she works full-time as a writer, photographer, crafter, and artist. She can be found in her garden studio testing new soap recipes and creating beautiful things with natural elements. As a Master Gardener, she volunteers with a school-to-farm program that teaches inner-city children how to grow and cook their own food.

At the end of the day, Stephanie enjoys every moment she can get with her family. She lives with her husband, son, and tiny dog, who provide her with inspiration and delight both in and out of the garden.

Books by Stephanie Rose

See all of the books at: https://gardentherapy.ca/books/

Garden Made: A Year of Seasonal Projects to Beautify Your Garden & Your Life

The Garden Therapy Coloring Book Printable PDF

Get Growing! Expert Seed Starting for the DIY Gardener

Good Clean Fun: THE Idea Book for Creative Melt and Pour Soap Projects

The Natural Beauty Recipe Book: 45 Easy-to-Make Skincare Recipes for the Whole Family (eBook version)

Sugar and Spice: 40+ Handmade Gifts from the Kitchen

Printed in Great Britain
by Amazon

50329008R00034